Dirt Roads

For Neil and Keith, who know where they are.

John Davies
Dirt Roads

seren

seren is the book imprint of
Poetry Wales Press Ltd
2 Wyndham Street, Bridgend, Wales, CF31 1EF

A CIP record for this title is available
from the British Library

ISBN 1-85411-184-1

*The publisher works with the financial support of the
Arts Council of Wales*

Cover image: 'Arrival' by Maredudd ab Iestyn, 1995

Printed in Palatino
by The Cromwell Press Ltd, Melksham

Contents

7   Gold

8   Sheriff

9   A Cave

10   The Underground Store

11   The Quarry

13   Lift That

15   Bikers

16   Where You Are

18   Footprints

19   Mr. Roberts

20   Cottonwood Waltz

21   Borrowing the Mauser

23   The News from Tokyo

24   My Brother Keeps Moving

26   Casting

27   Braveheart

28   Walking the Line

30   The Job

32   At Carver's Place

33   The Disappeared

34   Bluegrass

35   Sources

36   Views from the Workshed

43   Ray's Birds

45   Charles Tunnicliffe

46   Sea, Headland, Clouds

48   Silting

49   A Short History of
       the North Wales Coast

50   Talacre's Big Sleep

51   Missionaries

52   Portmeirion

53   Climbing with the Wrong Person

54   Lord Penslate's Castle

55   Riders, Walkers

56   Reading the Country
56   I. Sentences while remembering
56   II. The lost kingdom
57   III. An old thing
57   IV. Cwmorthin
58   V. The fisherman
58   VI. Captain John Huws
                of the *Oriana*
59   VII. The weathercock
59   VIII. Barrenness
60   IX. The pylon
60   X. The moment
61   XI. The old language
61   XII. Penmon
62   XIII. Llyn y Gadair
62   XIV. Bits and pieces
63   R.S. Thomas
65   Biography
66   Poet on Tour
67   Emptying the Lake
68   Mountains, Valleys

Gold

Whatever the place is called,
"isolation" it's pronounced.
The dirt road
is a ghost hunt by a snake.

When gold showed up,
people grabbed it and ran.
Things keep running,
all down.
Though the sign says *Pop. 12,*
the old man thinking
hard with both hands
makes it nine. Or ten.
He recalls meat so tough
his fork stuck in the gravy,
"a loyal two-woman man"
with an eye for the frame house
recently abandoned.
One day it could be his.

Patched by movers-on,
the place looks stunned.
Back there under a cloth
and tin box marked *Cutlery*
is a table
somebody did not return to.
One day it will be yours.

But just off the road,
set in tangled water:
stones which, held up at arm's length,
were skylights
fresh from being undervalued.

So what if none were nuggets,
flecks in the urgent flow?
Dirt roads assay their worth.

Sheriff

When silver was found, a few of the boys
got married in the excitement,
wiped out the last Indian
then named the town after him.
The sunlit river beating drums
still has silver going for it.
But spoilheaps yield scrub.

Sheriff's in competition with
his health. A single-barrelled stare
tracks bored teenagers, hormones
on fire, his son might inherit
if he returns from California.
Beyond cars, trails shrug off
the emptied slopes and climb.

The past's hard on this place.
In a shack years back, he found
bleached newsprint turn to Moscow snow:
two German generals marched,
heads unbowed, with beaten troops
as if the shack had to store
a reason for staying upright.

Rock, shimmering, squats in wait.
Sometimes a waterfall of light
pours off a ledge. Its overspill
is his road between Elkhorn and Duchesne
which, though hazed like
anything too near to be in focus,
has veins of pure glitter.

Haze lingers. Travellers bring their own.
Straight roads can't shake loose
what keeps narrowing the gaze —
but they try, they track the sun.
Surrounded by your car, just
once you glimpsed him, brushed
by the moment's shine that lit you also.

A Cave

it seems, with pools broken open silver
when roofdrops hit. But what has painted
high on the wall ochre chains and fur
is rust. Bolts have orange pelts. Fainter,
moss crawling after light along hacked shelves
halts at a tunnel. Floodwater has drowned
its plankwalk trodden as if for ever,
floated just out of reach. And bearing down
like outer space is the dense curved weight
on things given up half-used though not
from choice in this little globe, dictating
how few remnants survive stopped
ways of life turned suddenly inside out.
The one cave world and you are in its mouth.

The Underground Store

Near the Swansea mine, in foothills
south of Salt Lake, he cut down cedars.
He excavated by night. Then lined walls,
covered wood supports and the roof
with desert clay. And? Silverware,
cut crystal, china gleamed above hardware
and crowds at the underground store
that, with Ivor and Morgan, his boys,
William Ajax built out of the sun in 1873,
eleven thousand cool square feet.

It's a pit now. Stumps, sprinkled glass.
Time's light-fingered. But under the scrub
run dream tunnels from a country riddled.
Where is the buried Cathedral? Slaughterhouse?
Where does Jacob's Ladder clamber from slate
to sea? Llechwedd. Cwmorthin. Chwarel Hên.
Chains hang from work unfinished
over rusted drills. Echoing, shafts speak
louder than men who, not profiting much,
drove deep into giant pockets.

Way down in space are halls, stairs,
bridges, as if slate were hardened lava,
or hollows the moulds for a great city
waiting. As if the fit young dead
of world wars had built sepulchres from air.
As if people sick of lowness, undermining it,
dug deep to construct in brutalist rococo
an underworld haunting what we have made
of higher ground. Dust blows under doors
still from the underground store.

The Quarry

Out on the ridge,
I checked the incline
to a row of sheds
leaning on each other.
Dead-ends. No sign

but I slid down anyway
past winding gear.
Clear on a wall,
these scratched words:
"I am not here".

Glanced up. That close,
a slate tip collapses
avalanching, stopped
for just seconds
to let feet pass.

Remains of a still-warm
fire could be anyone's,
candle stubs too.
Walkers get everywhere
though I'd passed none.

I checked the shaft,
swam on my feet, eyes
gone, down sides
sucking me through
trickling ricochets

till it split,
it forked, I could feel.
Stopped. Couldn't turn.
Which of us, which
one's the quarry?

A breeze. Light
as if someone yanked
a door then stood
aside. I edged out
on rails. Hacked

slopes. On an upturned
wagon, scrawled,
was "This is not the way".
Move on. Feet
clattered the rockfall.

Sky was a lid.
Walls gathered round,
forcing more stone
down a crammed
mouth in the ground.

I reached the rim,
unplugged my boots
and grass slid me
out through open sky
the fastest route.

Lights, a dream begun
without me. My pack
creaked, bringing
the mountain down.
I said when I got back:

"There's no one there".
It didn't take long
filing my report.
Next day I checked it.
Someone had scrawled "Wrong".

Lift That

Tonight I thought of the old man, seventy,
my uncle who worked with his son-in-law
in a dead-end shaft, just them, dragging
slate from the wreckage. Only
twelve years back. It seems a lot more.

Even eating, sometimes when I'd pass
off-duty, they seemed apart. Strange how
sandwiches need watching. The old one
would answer, both say nothing. Partners?
I couldn't believe them, towing

slate on cracked wagons through the gloom
where only water was going on
and on, when the lit town below
had everything. Except workroom.
They were like fossils trying to shed rock.

I know this, it was cold. The old man
called me Sarge. The other bothered me
and, once, I saw him stride from a shaft
with a big green slab in his arms.
He dumped it smack at my uncle's feet.

"Lift that," he said (I'm translating now),
"then criticize. I'll treat her how I please."
It seemed to me the old man hauled
silence mostly. He'd changed. Anyhow,
I didn't go back up there for weeks.

Then, "The young one's gone," someone said.
When I visited my uncle, notebook
shut, at his house dragged from the quarry,
his room had just got out of bed,
tools everywhere, wet clothes, boots.

"Said he was going. Good riddance."
Nor was his daughter, streets away, upset.
That was that. People talk though, even
gossip's checked on the off-chance —
we had to put on a show. I won't forget

our lads strung out in macs, a Wednesday
harvest across half a mile of slate,
rain, slate. It was pointless,
and cold weather put the dogs off. Anyway,
"He'll be home again in weeks, you wait".

Days later, it dawned. Could be. Sweating,
I climbed to the quarry in full kit,
levered that green slab the younger one
had hauled, and started scraping.
Him. It was him. Then I replaced it.

Bikers

At the village with no car park,
slate's lava flow was in place
of second homes.
A band of conifers sneaked
out over the hill.

All afternoon, the hang-glider
circling like a kite
turned kidnapper had threatened,
unless the place paid
some attention, to let go.

But frames couldn't straighten.
A bad case of extraction's
rictus, how could it look up?

Down the incline hiccuped by ruts,
bickering, two dirt bikes droned,
groping to pick up din.
Then shrilled flat out
through dust barriers smashed in the blast
past sheds, a burnt car —
two of grit's thousands
grinding the crater's edge.

Retake workspace, deny
waste. Take chances not helmets.
Wreckage you're always heading for
and can't fly from
fill roaring with yourself.

Where You Are

I

For Billy Rice of Blaenau Ffestiniog

What to do with slate or life but shape it?
Carved before your time, in Dyffryn Ogwen
are starbursts in shelves, and birds inhabit
mantelpieces. Now edges curve again:

turned on your homemade lathe, mossgreen,
that bowl slid from bed unbroken. Its base,
rough proof of origin, deepens the sheen
of your part discovery, part rescue.

A zodiac at Tregarth lights a fireplace.
Time shimmers. Folk the art schools never knew
assert what television screens deny
outright: what you have is where you are.
Turn to reflect light from an inner sky.
Find rock shining clear as a lodestar.

II

For Peter Prendergast of Deiniolen

Up on the slope, two boys were ferreting.
What slipped down eager as bad news again
was emptying warrens as I climbed the lane
to your studio, from winter into spring.

The fuse from boyhood's coalscape, underground,
had ignited canvas. Slate country flared
with you, blasts of colour from midair
sparking hollows, in land that seemed newfound.

I had thought such colours too bright. Today
near Llanberis though, from a shaft that turned
ice black then burst on an open spillway,
I saw it, an explosion of wet fern.

Angle of entry is all. The ravine
is dark. I wish you multitudes of green.

Footprints

O.S. maps are fine except in forestry
where paths breed then forget,
having trees to get to, trees to see.

Each seemed the least travelled by.
They made no difference till one
gave me a shot of field and sky.

Rhiwddolion was not lost. Sprawled
houses measured the distance
between forestry and stone walls

where doorways wide enough to say
"They've gone" had ferns on mantelpieces,
draped boughs of another washday,

flicker on burned-out hearths.
Slate slabs crossed a field
like giant footprints: the one path

still went to chapel, straight.
By the time I left, there was just
that well-heeled shine of slate.

Conifers loomed. Keeping confidence
intact through shadowy twists
and times takes a lot of ignorance.

Mr. Roberts

A city rigged with mountains:
past his house on Fifteenth Street
schooners skated the Pacific, sun
on the wooden lighthouse flashed.
Streets wore bunting that year
Roosevelt visited when Indians
traded pieces of ore for food.

>   *He had known a hill dive*
>   *in the river, its slate overspill*
>   *his garden. Was it he'd*
>   *buried years in the candled dark,*
>   *watched people became engines?*
>   *On Bethesda's shattered ribcage,*
>   *one track had spread a web.*

Afloat one spring, he heard
a hailstorm seethe: packed shoals
shoved the boat, fishsurf, fishspray.
And with a big crowd once, he saw —
held till the gas puffed it
to full bloom — a white balloon
fly men like seeds blown clear.

>   *After men had marched in tune*
>   *with the band's brass necks,*
>   *swerved, blown both managers out,*
>   *echoes went recruiting.*
>   *Propped roofs were scored*
>   *with harder sounds, strike, strike.*
>   *Till poverty struck back.*

He worked and bought, and he lived
alone. His heart moved up and down
with the price of silver.
Gifts he gave short shrift.
When he died, they found under
earth, rocks, piled in the numbed
house, his tunnel with one chair.

Cottonwood Waltz

They held dances at the schoolhouse.
No roof. Here's the door.
Someone's tried to fix
holes stomped in the floor.

Sagebrush out in the baseball cage
swings through its own heat,
pretty pattering
of someone with light feet.

Arms sway. Given fresh wind,
a tough scratchy band
of cottonwoods strikes up.
It looks like hands

would link if only the school door
out of the skyblue
would open and there stand —
Someone would know who.

Borrowing the Mauser

for Rich

"Let's shoot," he says,
the ex-trumpet player parachuted
out of adolescence to Vietnam.
His head plays solo still.
So will he...?
"Buy a trumpet? Practise a little,
pretty soon you'll want to join a band.
If you're not careful,
you could end up happy."

We visit his father's place.
Wesley of the intrepid socks,
recoiling from retirement,
has bought a stump grinder
or metal Sumo grunting.
On building lots, shredding
what's left of trees,
it roots out the old, makes space
for brandnew walls.

Wesley has his Mauser.
The yellow stock kept polished
in memory of D-Day
gleams, its muzzle a clean whistle.
And shells? Over the tabletop,
he fires a brass burst
then claws back half.

Though green's making up lost ground
at the mine brooding
on spent bricks and shells,
metal would keep its edge
if it could, every bar and strut.
Wire grips snapped fence-posts,
figuring what to keep, how
much it's better to give up.

We two press against the recoils.
Blasts blank thought.
Can't see our hits, too far,
and there are still shells left
when he says, "That's it",
heads back to the car.

I smoke. He flicks the tape,
Nat Adderley. Whose trumpet's
soaring clears the air, branches
then leaves
itself and reforms like
a tree fluttering
the sun to small bright pieces.

The News from Tokyo

I stayed with my brother in New York.
He was caretaking for Mrs. Minami,
Tokyo millionairess, who'd left
her favourite colour.
Florid porcelain, bureaux,
winged chairs, angels everywhere,
were pink in the style of Louis
the Predictable.
Our voices echoed and rococoed.

In Tokyo, money had dried up —
faxes arrived, stuttering,
the phone a question mark.
Gareth plugged holes
but rain kept nosing in.
Fake covings flaked
on walls an unhealthy rouge,
on Mrs. Minami's aim to "Wrap
a Pink Ribbon Around the World".

A veldt of carpeting kept
feet off the ground.
Around homespun talk,
silks rustled that weren't ours.
Sweat worked when air conditioning
would not.

In three acres, while cicadas
zipped and unzipped trees,
boulders like slabs of old
testament kept growing.
And stone showed through inside,
pink rinsing out, the place
groping back to basics
as we'd have to also
if we remembered what they were.

My Brother Keeps Moving

and sometimes I catch up.
Where he had paused,
green slopes dissolved in the lake
that for now absorbed him too.
His rented house,
inch by inch, was sliding
but a hummingbird buoyed the porch.
Over our heads,
branches exchanged leaves.

Canada geese had landed.
Though they were nests
feathered by ripples, cloud
flashed just behind each eye
and they practised moonshots.
Their wakes electrified
branches not the one turtle.
A globe living in itself,
why would it need elsewhere?
The lake winked when it dived
deep among twisted roots
that were skeletons of whirlpools.

We fished later, no crossed lines.
The moon stared down
like a face which sees itself
in a mirror, the moon behind.
Where stillwater had netted
a fluster of stars, I watched
how light that fills up hours
moving boulders paints them out.
Couldn't tell water from the trees,
fell to swimming in leaves.

But Gareth kept at it, casting.
Soon he'd be off, another trip home.
And I recalled the hummingbird:
as if from a sprinkler,

one droplet had slipped
the common arc to spark its own,
make light of gravity, fly back
to feed on where it came from.

Between flight and stillness,
hovering, he raised his rod,
took aim.

Casting

Past the weir where steelwater
milled to a sheen
splinters, Gareth is teaching
his five-year-old to fish.
His line is straight.
The late sun salts it,
white thread over fires.

Sudden rinses, slaps.
The current's muscle flexes
so he hands the boy his rod.
Under whose arm it seems a fence-post
bucks when, reeling, he levers
silver — he's out of himself
downline, dive, scramble.

And water thrown for the light
to catch
sprays through spread fingers,
fumbled glitters
brightest as they fall.

He flaps slack line.
Turns, blank, to his father.
How can he know
there will be other bass,
netted, bulging with this hour?

Braveheart

Stranded in middle age,
he couldn't decide,
Doug from Carolina,
of Welsh and Scots ancestry,
which to follow up.
Till he watched Hollywood's
pipe fantasia, *Braveheart*.
No contest. So he signed
for a tartan weekend
then bought the kilt.
And modelled it for me.

Why should I smile?
Not just a country big enough
to get lost in, small ones
dream fallback positions.
Rumours of dark
Celtic roots in Iberia
feed bright thoughts.
Doug might know where
the Welsh-Spanish hang out
or where (I have the legs)
I'd find a bullfighter's cape.

Walking the Line

From one tie to another,
every pace or three
you jump to keep in step.
Or fast-track a rail
bright over sleepers —
and lose balance, energy.
The whole thing
that keeps coming to a point
doesn't make it.

At the fishing bridge,
among struts beneath the line
I glimpse the small grill
Hiroshi uses to cook bass.
It gleams, a hidden
shrine to the wide river
loosening day's grip on him.
When I step off,

stones break into grass.
Sun in another country
is a different sun.
Free for the first May
in a working life,
I feel workable, hearing
the tidal river run,
watching breakers rise and
falter to remind the tide,

touched by driftwood washed
from rigidity into waves.
Let it keep coming,
come what may.
And what's too good to last
doesn't need to, doubt
just a tributary of this surge
within, deep inland,
that can always charge itself.

Among sumac, cottonwoods,
swampland resists paths.
Green's sucked me in
with the jay head up
from the puffed roost of itself.
Still though I hear
each passing train's insistent
whatever your theme is,
better make it work.

I'll follow the treeline
that might take me
along the creek to Tivoli.
But not yet waterbound,
I shall return downline.
Straight metal
defines free flow —
I need to keep this other way
fresh, and working.

The Job

for Bob

Floundering at low tide
to brace your wharf with beams,
we'd scraped deep pits
mud tried to fill with water.
Trees built a heat canopy.

Hard work. Well, yours was,
whipping concrete in a barrow
into cream, no sweat.
"Look," you said, sharp
as I fished around. It was

like being given a job.
Where two slant currents
arrowed the running sun,
a heron stalked its own
rifle through a melodrama.

You filled both pits,
levered in place the beams
that I helped screw.
And we watched Oro Bay tilt
slowly, filling up the creek.

Closer, the heron's shimmied
dance was making light
of mud. When it stopped
to pierce its reflection, now
there was good fishing

to be had, word and line,
in our three ways
of sharpening effort's point.
It lifted. A contraption
of bones and feathers,

the heron clambered, flew
as if a hinge swung the sky
ajar to let in air, kept
swinging it open easily, shut.
Then left it wide open.

At Carver's Place

Mouth open,
the gaunt waitress is pouring
herself into a barrel,
the big man who seems
to take it all in.
Soon there are just hands waving.
Too much.

She watches him reach his car:
framed behind plate glass,
he might get clearer.

She stands.
She starts to collect
herself. Is still starting
as she upends his cup
and nothing falls out.

All you can say about divorce,
she tells no one, is
you chose right, guessed wrong.

The Disappeared

Montgomery Place commands
the river and much else.
Our helpful guide's precise:
"In eighteen twenty-four,
the native Americans here
disappeared". Melted
by fabrics, gilt, paint, heat,
we spill out on the lawn.

Dis-appeared. The disappeared:
how did a past participle
fade through adjective
to end up as a noun?
Strange process. As in
"wilderness" become "gardens".
The raw Catskills leap
in haze beyond a pergola.

Tight paths encircle trees
where shadows break cover,
cross lawns and shrubbery,
vanish. Trellises appear.
Borders are trim, no weeds.
What are weeds though
but displaced flowers?
It depends who —

"Disappeared", officials claim.
The rest say, "the disappeared".
Now that sun is fading
gold afternoon into dusk,
cool's ending up as chill.
Darkness is not just air.
All around are buried
verbs, the made-to-disappear.

Bluegrass

A foggy mountain breakthrough, sun's all-change
    slow orange blossom special
    for the bluegrass festival

at Trefriw arrived panting late on time.
    Fiddles scribbled, rhymed tightly.
    Riddling mandolins made sleights

of handshake into gusts whose upbeat blew
    hair strewn from bandanas. Feet
    bumpstarted Spring. Its jump greeted

rhythms bounced from upcountry states cockeyed,
    buoyed higher as vibrating
    double basses dug deep, straight

through a Sunday when shadow spires of trees
    retreated in sun's crossfire.
    And everything conspired

to sing the place itself careening split
    orbits suddenly between
    sky-blueness and grassgreen.

Sources

Sometime I'd like to go to Crisfield, Maryland,
where "two dumb old country boys" with a barber's shop
saved themselves for other business to hand:
carved birds, imagination's airdrop

out of cleared skies. All they borrowed from was memory.
Their decoys' upswept bills, cocked heads, are records
of how life drawn to art takes off again, how teals,
canvasbacks and pintails become Wards.

Would I find things changed there on Chesapeake Bay?
You bet. What beckons though like a country road:
the illusion that where men lived is halfway
to how they saw. Which can be borrowed.

West in poet Hugo's steps years back, I tried placing
him at the Skagit, as if that darkly running song,
his secret, still floated. Cold water. Why trace
the source when a river is so long?

He'd left Port Townsend too. It was a waterspout,
flung arcs of ferries everywhere, sending —
with drops at Bremerton, Seattle — right out
to the Pacific then infinity the town's end.

To locate is to limit glittering lines of contact.
Best open yourself, not haunt abandoned yards.
Still, words are not wood. His poem "The Swimmer at..."
Sometime I'd like to see Lake Edward.

Views from the Workshed

I

Quick. A squirrel
launching the glider of its tail
flies up a trunk.

I watch what my hands
make of bandsawn wood.
Not much usually
though hands don't know that,
and anyway even our apple tree
flares only once a year.
Twisting, it can't untie its knot.

But it gives rise to birds, gives rise.
Carved birds too want to live,
blocked wings become wing blur,
heads turn to their shadows.
How to grasp what flies?

Catch, say, the dark star trilling
before it is a skylark.

II

Beyond trees: rooftopple
onto the sea murmuring
"Let's try it this way".

Shorebirds way down
at the damp edge
find windows with wandering seasons.

Even at rest, their shapes
fly through beaks
that are calling's arcs

till they disappear.
You try to follow,
taking wood, carving

liberties with the theme of S.
Shaping is all.
Finished things don't stir —

polish makes things shine,
yes, but polish seals them off.
These summer nights,

sea has a giant redwood disc
burn everything
then it's start again.

III

And another
I can't catch:
the raven of Moel Ddu
in its own sky,

that watches a path run
straight to the quarry.
Again it circles
the chapel's torn covers.

It will not follow
where streams weary
of light-splitting
idle their last laps.

It keeps, bearded, high
places. It ministers
to a quarry, lake,
a chapel that once

glimpsed souls fly up
so perfectly healed
no scars were visible.
And won't sink lower.

IV

I think of Wendell Gilley
whose eyes taking off
made sense
of what drives art to abstraction.

At Southwest Harbor, Maine,
the sea was high in branches
near the white gallery
where his birds had gathered.
I was years too late to meet him.
Didn't matter. Something
with claws, a frog-soft body
winged, the head a mallet,
had landed.
It could have swept earth's contours
through the air, beaten darkness senseless.
Bird in the wood. Wood in the bird.
Whichever way you looked at it,
his barn owl, you were looking up.

V

The Wasatch Whittlers' annual bash was packed.
"You wanna compete at the very top?"
Lance Krogue, guest speaker in a grizzled cap,
eyes clenched, hovered over us sadsacks.
"You need lessons: feathering and painting,
bird anatomy. Sharpen up — hey, look,
give it hunnert per cent. Why bet on luck?"
At that, even our braced shoulders pointed
up. Minds soared. The top called like a raven.
But you know how it is, the cosmic drag
of inertia gets in the hawk-eyed way
of thrust. Dust fell. Inspiration we flagged
at maybe ninety-five per cent, yep,
and persp- Anyway, it never added up.

VI

The sky is blank paper
I lean my mind on.

Something takes off, a flash
of desperation.
I type it anyway,
tapping at my shell,
some wordscape keen
to justify itself.

Last week a thrush
thudded against the glass.
So at least that's clear:
deception works both ways.

Outside, the yew tree
fingers splinters.
Unable to contain
its reds, it wants to break and go
whereas words are going nowhere.

I have this block of yew,
and a kestrel snatched from horizons
by my screwed-down branch
might do.

VII

Lots of ways, yes,
of getting it wrong.

Say early on
you lost proportion.

Or flaws you can't
smooth out join up.

Live into it:
things made from scratch

and scowl don't work.
How well you do

still counts when
it's what you have to do.

Symmetry's hard late on,
you get lopsided.

Overall,
carving's easier.

Ray's Birds

Lunchtime, the way he tells it,
with Ray weightless, orbiting
the forgotten planet Stress,
his chickens screech SOS
so he's off. Fox?
No, they're spun shuttlecocks
because just yards away
stands a sparrow-hawk — on a jay
quivering, spread to take the spike.
Ray drifts dreamlike.
When the hawk lifts and its full load
drags it down, he lunges, rolls
to save the jay, jaycrazy,
grabs a leg. And sits up. Dazed,
he's got the hawk. Flared eyes
flash beak. Ray makes —crabwise
past the pigeon loft, on wings —
for his shed, shuffles in, gets string,
gets stabbed, ties one leg to a brick towed
clattering. Leaps out. Shed explodes.

"So what now, Ray?" That's Rosalie,
unacquainted with falconry.
His arm with clenched fist
lifts. Air swoops, glory clamps his wrist.
"What'll it eat?" is Ray's sole doubt,
who spends days not finding out
then tries pigeon, desperate. It's his.
For the hawk another bloody quiz.
Chasing its eyes around, it picks
at the soft corpse, flicking
to feather it. And pecks. And tears
raw treasure — soon, compère
of the feast, Ray's killed another three.
His top racing birds look queasy.
The hawk though hops on his leather glove
to stare, his lethal turtledove.

Rosalie sums up, unflinching,
the whole strange thing:
"You've got to let it go".
The sky's big through that shed window,
Ray has had doubts. It's young,
so demandingly high-strung
he has no time to live in.
And he's running out of pigeon.
So he pulls the door, stands
back. Loud hoovering woodland,
an astonishment of light,
yank the fat bird right
through the cramped frame
of all that's tame
in the world of walls
out to a radiant, rayless windfall.

But Ray has wings still. Weeks later,
watching his fastest bird home straight
toward's Bishop's Wood,
he'd fly too if he could.
End of a race. His timer's ready, best
time, the loft a homemade nest.
Ray's eyes
are full of sky.
Then, higher, he sees it, black
cross, black skyjack.
That hawk tapping its wings on air
plummets, hits foursquare
his pigeon gone south
before Ray can close his mouth.
And a puff of brown
feathers filters down.
Ray's there like a praying mantis.
Don't tell him I told you this.

Charles Tunnicliffe

The last white of day is brushed through dark
blues into magpie almost not there.
Tunnicliffe painted it. This late, still in place.
Seeking exactness, he found art, let facts suggest
what could translate given time, shape, space,
into the ungiven that never rests.

The next page flutters. And, a whole clifftop
in its grip, his hawk with wings half-spread
is about to launch it. What seem models of restraint,
concise drawings started casual flights.
They were reference points with which paint
made free, of which a floating brush made light.

His mallards do with dignity what ducks do best,
upend it. Curlew like seaweed in the rain,
clumps of a khaki shore, await sky's outcome.
Such making stirs ours. Details inform the mind
so art can teach (fingers flex and drum) —
up to the point where art leaves information behind.

Sea, Headland, Clouds

for Megan

I stayed with my aunt
on her broad terraced street
that strolls a clifftop.
Nearsighted, eighty,
she retains what she needs.
"Oh, that's good," she'd say
of things I barely recognised
till I sensed her view.

Harbour tides built walls
that kept going under,
dragging their remnants back.
Sceptics, gulls prodded.
But her place looks out
on wings to the horizon,
blown hills leaving white
hair behind in valleys.

There's a headland too,
cleared site for remaking.
Trees frisked bare hang on.
Buffeted, stormproof,
rock scoured to roundedness
falls back on caves
as what seems firm
crumbles enough to last.

Returning at evening,
I'd tell her some of this.
She knew most of it already,
buoyant, having lived
by sea, headland, clouds.
One day, a flock of yachts
rode out the calm that turned
into her kitchen.

Mornings, she'd wave me off.
I watched waves polish
scalloped shells of bays
(two seals flickered
like shadows of big birds),
and farms sent fields
to sea, all down the coast
flags semaphoring green.

Silting

is going on, you can tell
by the stranded shore and jetty.
So marshland with channels coiled
slips to sea — stripped decks

take eyes and heart flat out
past coldwater farms hunched
in their whistling past
to where tides career unclouded.

The path winds round and back.
No horse waits in the field
of roofs opposite that house
with shell paths in its garden.

Who lives there? Not aunts, uncles,
ready with food (their word
for welcome) and the time
to open Gower bays. And, yes,

we have been here before.
I called once at Angle, boyhood
harbour of a friend; reflections
at his feet, he could walk on water.

High hedges, low sea. Nice place,
I told him later, but—
"Which way did you go?" he asked.
Wrong angle, south from middle age.

A Short History of the North Wales Coast

All right, agreed, just a low shelf
piled with hills. Still, it was itself —

incomprehensible come rain or war,
life folded, you'd say, in a bottom drawer —

till the railway's sudden drum
thundered "customers".

Bingo. Both sides across stunned ground
snuffled like truffle hounds.

Came a blue surge of matelots,
quaintesques, glee parties, pierrots,

and the Palace saw a real African kraal
stretch to gondolas on a canal.

St. David? Slept in magic groves a span?
Would have sold out, *Dave the Fasting Man.*

Here anyway in an early photo,
advert smart, a house on show

foreshadows what's all spick and spent.
It is the ghost of crisis present:

on her lawn like a Welcome mat,
a lady addresses a caged bird. Just that.

With the parrot though, so many
ears unlearned so much from opportunity

that tongues licked brandnew speech.
And all changed. Like that. It's teaching

time at Bagillt where our lady misrule
has started-up the Parrot School.

Talacre's Big Sleep

It's January.
Bungalows, chalets hunched
in the rain are suspects.
They know it, curtained,
peering out through keyholes,
caravans too
disguised as a wall of tin.

The cafe dead, one car
investigates.
Up the cracked road it goes
nowhere, stops where the tide
swills dirty macs.
And back.
There are three seagulls,
two men sharing
not a lot of hair.

Any leads at the Smuggler's Inn,
that hornpipe casualty?
Around bins, nettles
shake grey heads.

Back of the village,
feet up, pondering,
dunes slump on one another.
Gimme a light,
says the lighthouse.
The arcade without electric
schlock treatments
is not amused.

And you are the witness,
drawn again to the scene
of your own making.
What can you say,
"Arrest the rain"?

Missionaries

Past drifts of shoppers,
shops closed, the church wall
where leaning youths sip girls,
these two had climbed the hill
on active service from a town
I know. I asked them in,
nostalgic for belief or Utah.

One hid his light under a blush,
the other was open sky.
Both believed in the hilltop
where, for me, clouds hang flags
that keep getting blown away.
Neither would be sucked in
by my spiritual vacuum.

They had learned desert rules
and lived by them.
They did not stroll alone.
I thought of settlements
baked into solidarity
behind tough Brigham Young:
when a tree stirs, wind

races through his hair again,
jacket tightening in his fingers.
A big wind had borne
these two, aimed above
the cries of an uncertain
age, "No way! No Way!",
at a town scratched by gulls.

Glad for them, of them,
"I'll look at the Book of Mormon,"
I said as they left.
And half-believed I might.
It was late. Cars on our hilltop
were sweeping again, searchlights
keen in the unblinking dark.

Portmeirion

Cloud has new domes to deliver,
the estuary (when it can stir
itself) water for islands
to be dipped in shine. Stream
slippages show how earth dreams
too, gleams packed in sand

plumped by tides full of elsewhere.
Wings, scattering, assert airy
claims that there's no fixed place
in the curved world's spun
spray of easy transformations.
From the hill, floating them in space,

this village or pastel fountain
spills bright things born again.
And its weather-vane points firmly
everywhere in the play
of light on stone via Fabergé
and Llŷn by way of Italy

that is nowhere, says the piazza's
line of gilded dancers so far
from Siam. Roofs reel. Hereabouts
are follies. This one's riches caught
forever on the wing are the rare sort:
brought in for once, not shipped out.

Climbing with the Wrong Person

Greenscapes terminally beautiful wince
welcome. They know him. They've known him since
he started talking. Wind fiddled
with metal sheds back there, sheep stirred
slate xylophones. Both half-heard.
Irritated, a hiccuping grouse slid
off. I can't. What it is, he has become
his missing Walkman. There's space to fill —
so air swells as the packed coast spills
through him its chatter, even wind struck dumb
at the shaft where questions took their toll.
"What did you expect, a ladder?
Some trainee rockman with his dad?"
I knew what could have filled that hole.

A boulder waited like an owl upstairs
over Llyn Geirionydd. One swoop, that's all.
Or the muscular, brown-armed waterfall
could have bent and.... Hell, nature doesn't care.
He won't switch off and it's miles from here,
miles, the burial mound at Tomen-y-Mur.

Lord Penslate's Castle

From a mile off, his quarries emptied
into it. The Great Hall
on two levels smudged
by candles was a vault
only boldest echoes measured.
Carvings spidered
crisp arches spanning
tunnels. Around one:
a row of human hands.

Drills, powder, gouged out chambers.
Shafts became chimneys,
tramways hauled fresh
water on its knees
to the castle's foot. Having built,
he furnished it.
On slate turned, shelved,
peeled to fine paper,
he wrote himself.

Slate flowed into clocks, into cabinets.
Squeezed from its last
memory of oxides:
sweat-stained glass.
Exhaustion sighed. At last, hammering
became sonatas on a slab
fine-tuned to walnut,
a powder charge those great
doors banged shut.

The news resounded in high places.
Prince Pückler-Muskau,
Victoria, Gladstone, stayed.
The public come now.
They move in single file through shafts
of light adrift
with dust that's yet
too fine to raise a cough,
that will not settle.

Riders, Walkers

Damp, cold, dust? They were for the pack.
For one man in 1939, arriving on horseback
with his company, air conditioning was installed.
Swept slate caverns at Manod became halls
when Charles I, painted by Van Dyck, was stored
out of bombing range with London's hoard.
He looks grand still, unsurprised to be around.
The quarrymen, alas, stay underground.
But in the National Interest, common sense
says things of value must take precedence.
Think of the painting that you value
most. Walkers give way to riders. Which are you?

They had their place in the picture, cold, damp,
for Mary E. Thompson at this time. Cramped
by ill-health, she leant ambition's ladder up as far
as the Brussels Academy but surfaced in Bethesda.
From a split block, a small cloud of dust
escapes; a pencil can feel rock's upthrust.
She walked, climbed, and for almost twenty
years the galleries she toured were quarried,
sheet after sheet, as pale drawn workday
faces against stone in all the colours of grey
defied mass. In time, she could tell them who,
when they asked, pointing, "Pwy 'di'r un acw?"*

So here is Alun Jones, blacksmith, concentrating
down a studious nose. Will Proudley cutting slate.
Here is the art of shaded surfaces, its value
that record sparked revelation. Not high art, true,
but true not low. Part of the story
half-buried still, it redefines nobility —
like the slate bust of Gwilym Hiraethog, icon
of nonconformity detached from the salon
at Penrhyn Castle (and carved by?), firebrand
snuffed by the country of the bland.
In a cluttered glass case: the fate
of art, shown to an antechamber, in an unfree state.

* Who's that one there?

Reading the Country

I. Sentences while remembering

"I'm going to paint," she said, "your portrait".
But turned up proudly apologetic
with this townscape she'd held back from the Tate.
North or south, yes, I recognised it: slicks
of wet slate, where the hills pull up to brood
on drainage, spell out opposites of wealth.
The Welfare. The cafe molesting food.
Stoned houses. Just the chemist's shines with health,
not good, and Bethania, falling apart
since takeaways dawned, offers carpets cheap.
Grey magic. A paintsong sung by heart
to the tune *Doomed Rhapsodies of Sheep,*
it was all mine. She shrugged. "I'll do your head
next," she promised. "You've done it," I said.

II. The lost kingdom

"Money," they answered him, the old pair roused
as if by a mansion grown from seed. Young
enough to bend, he tramped farmlight till spined
slopes fattened into valley. A big house
wallowed in shrubbery. He daydreamed. Sprung,
a smoothed passage took him in. Rockshine's
hoard of promises looked damp where he found
there was no door so he tapped, hammered, kept
on, hooded in candlesmoke, heard spellbound
his quarryings harvested. They were swept
to a tinkle of glass on the slate wall's
other side. The wall never thinned. Farmland
dreamed him, under its crown of thorns. A fall
of light, late on, showed him his ancient hands.

III. An old thing

He'll, listen, wheeze like a busted sofa.
Then that matchbox rustling in his chest
ignites. Jesus. He's his village, depressed,
a quarry worked-out, the last railcar
from Llanberis a century away
from our coastal town, and now he's stopped.
At the old folks' home near the video shop,
he's not dressing or undressing slate today.

It was a war so they slept in barracks,
men against rock. He caught fleas, lost an eye —
not a dry one in the house, all flak
the way he tells it. A life cabin'd, clearly
gone. All that stuff about *cabanau*.
Still, you wish he'd not asked, "What's your story?"

IV. Cwmorthin

It has emptied, that bowl of a valley
hung cracked in Blaenau's draughty rafters, true.
It isn't empty now. Some rework slate.
And the new roads that make all secrets free
send weekend ski jackets glittering through
along paths half a century out of date.

A while back, the mute chapel's disbelief
flared white into graffiti: *Twll din
pob Sais* and *FWA*. They're fading though.
Trails thicken. It stares like the old chief —
scarfaced, somewhere innocent of wheels
till foraging newcomers cast shadows —
who asked how many, how many more are...?
and the answer was, "Like the stars".

V. The fisherman

The path tightroped over metal rubbish
fell in a tarn of gleaming liquid slate
more likely to hold fossils than fish.
Eager, he came over to the sluicegate,
young man, rod bouncing as his wet line winked.
And, accent not at home, chatted. Lately
he'd been dabbling. "Any in here, d'you think?"

Right out of luck, work, he deserved this time
better than the truth. It was spring. "Could be,"
I said, and waved as I started to climb.

Near the big house's shell, rhododendrons
bursting their marquee of pines rushed high
up the incline. Rails were rust ladders stunned,
pointing at a quarryful of sky.

VI. Captain John Huws of the *Oriana*

Who? Oh, some ghost here at the marina.
Let's say Davy Jones's locker-cleaner
raised on the local diet of hard rain,
muttering a dying language, Earstrain.
Kill that outboard anyway, get a fix
on lunch. Scramble-up some electronics.

End up as him? Listen, you'd have to be
reefed on sharp memories and all at sea,
give way to God not cabin cruisers, rid
yourself of weekend doldrums, wife and kids,
have sailed tall ships to San Francisco
from Porthmadog or through hell to Rio.

And still be back in time, a bit leaner,
to watch you navigate the marina.

VII. The weathercock

After Glyndŵr struck, grass sprang in the streets,
where deer grazed. Now all that's behind the town
whose quarries are shrouded in forestry.
Ignore the big hotel's recent breakdown,
shops for sale, demented peacocks shrieking
at Llanrwst. But does its castle (occupied)
belong to it or does...? Which tongue to speak?

Difficult. All manoeuvres must be deft.
Hovering, even the bridge can't decide
which is the Conwy's right bank and which left.
No wonder the weathercock's in a twist.
These days it recalls, airing its tall tail,
a favourite son, the one Welsh nationalist
peer of the English realm in all of Wales.

VIII. Barrenness

for Kyffin Williams

Best of all your paintings at Oriel Môn
I liked that figure in a rockscape. Sky's
going one way, the man another (down),
and mountains after him heave black stone,
mad as thunder. He is elderly, spry.
He is about to leave the frame or drown.

Now a trained English eye might take this chap
for Everyman in a painted sermon
on barrenness, all you need ever know.
But names matter: in coat and damp, flat cap,
this is *Dafydd Williams on the mountain*.
It's one moment, place. One life. And for now —
rained on, grimly passing through his portrait
homeward-bound — Dafydd wants out of it.

IX. The pylon

i.m. R. Williams Parry

It stood up. It flashed, whistled, as your hare
escaped, grass-mirrored streaks. Now pylons
seem (that was the thirties?) local hardware,
suspension bridges between then and now.

Last year near Melynllyn under white-capped
hills you'd know, a pygmy deer played come-gone,
swerved, jumpstopped, became two hares. Somehow
they had earth mapped, crazy with grasslaid traps

as it is. These days, what comes overhead,
that falls and is nowhere everywhere, weighs
heavier. Trees know. And water, lakes stunned
way down by such pourings on clean beds
of impure streams. If you could — Anyway,
this cannot be swerved from or outrun.

X. The moment

Way down in the giant bran tub plundered
of its treasure, overburdened ledges
still tipped, painstaking, filling the water.
Dead end. But a boy shuffled to its edge,
leading two flippered divers with their tanks.
Who became, billowing face-down, airmen
with baggy arms and legs outspread, then sank
as their whirlpools parachuted open

to a flooded world. Stone ruins inlaid
with mud. Maybe a tramline broken down,
one truck, its rust-wrapper flaking away.

And one survival: the sound breathing makes
like language under pressure, almost drowned
but strong close up, echoing in their wake.

XI. The old language

is yours if your word for home means "here".
Whatever it nudges from retirement,
sharp-eyed, beckons lost worlds words nearer.
It makes more connections than were meant.

Streams clear the throats of derelict caves
to deliver rivers that have outgrown
ruin fluently in slate villages,
in towns that are mills still dressing the flow.
Here is not home and doesn't sound (riches
pour past!) much like my country. But it is.

Echoes outlast sound. Listen, nudged awake,
they too murmur. Says earth's vocabulary
of names on scribbled surfaces, it takes
more than the one tongue to speak a country.

XII. Penmon

for Ieuan Wyn

We left the quarry town still tunnelling.
Roofless, men roofed cities with what they'd found.
What were they looking for? Where the Straits swing
open, it seemed far off, that ripped headland
whose priory also broke new ground.
I'd have your poem translated, I said.

In uncrowded air, a buzzard wavered,
casually tightrope walking. Then flew on
through your language and mine blurred
wordless in the skimming towards Penmon
as if rock's undertow had been washed green
of the faults words still try fathoming, thrown
by the eye over so much space between
us, so much spanning it, above, below.

XIII. Llyn y Gadair

i.m. T.H. Parry-Williams

Near the freed schoolhouse smoking at Rhyd-ddu,
a slate track still wanders off towards work,
feet thick, over boggy ground. It's a quay
by now: someone has launched into the murk
a Morris Minor where barbed wire, too, dives.
No wonder crowds at Beddgelert choose
a past well-crafted. So little survives,
the plot thins. Why pause? Something though moves.

Not two dry quarries crumbling like snow
on a straggle of thirsty conifers,
nor even the lone fisherman towing
his shoal of ripples round the lake. What stirs:
their belonging, stubborn greys, washed browns,
to a dead man's vision not closed down.

XIV. Bits and pieces

Why speak of such things? Because, under news
of the airports' pearly culture eased
through opalescent screens, plain voices say
what joins-up hills is more than just the view.
Because hills blur. Now eyes can't see the trees
for Hollywood, crammed ears turn the way
of the jogger soundproofed against spring.

Dead poets, tracks of the quarrymen, lakes
mining silver — why dabble in such things?
Because the living river of them slakes
now with then. Strongest in ground fractured,
it can flow speechless underground, go slack,
and mistrusts most the fluorescent sea.
But it runs on, pulling-in the country.

R.S. Thomas

I

Some comfortable harbour, say,
tugs a boat like its own
from the sea. Moored,
strangeness brings the storm.

Nights flicker.
And there is the manse's attic
blown, one curtain,
a lighthouse marvelling
at the bouncing moon.

II

We stood accused
of reading him. Wrong
language, place, wrong century.
Though his shadows from the fields
match ours, he made his own world,
lashed it for not surviving.
Which way forward but back?
His territory only boulders
gripped like knuckles.
It was shrinking always.
Rage kept him reinforced
until, falling short
of himself in the light
that language cannot span,
he saw a rimless world
extend the gifted heart's idea
of self, which is poetry.

III

Wind in the throes of turning
sighs that we have no centre.
He is our capital of echoes.

Places we find ourselves
not often, store voices far
from aerials turned to base —

one voice can set the whole
wood calling. And one wood asks
how earth and the planets

hang together, trees lit
by a bright field,
mild locals in eternity.

He reaped necessities:
dreams, with slant light
through our crowded sleep.

Our harvest, waking beyond
pylons skewering the hills,
is new land opened.

Biography

Larkin was here.
Space where he stood, no warm
neighbourhood,
why should
perspired guesswork fill? His
words will.

From the switched
-on underground of sense
float sounds
of a lone
instrument whose wry muted
blues

took
Hull-bent flights of
understatement
clear
of his own heartbeat, past
One-End Street

where he made
all separate blown notes
inseparable,
to shiver
high windows where we lie.
He chose

words, space,
clarity. *Open up that wonder*
and hear.
What
sang him has let him be
song only.

Poet on Tour

As if in some cupboard he's found
himself, spellbound,
he holds workshops
on himself with poems for props,
beams apology others cannot
be him driving from Camelot
in performance kit
with his *Caution: Poetry in Transit*
to pluck them off the shelf
for excursions around himself.
They are few, he's many.
Empty spaces? Hardly any
in sterile halls
where he plants his mobile bookstall
that a voice cannot fill.
The echo is hope's overspill.

And what can they give in return
for his love of myth, his heart-burn,
his "myriad obsessions" roaming
less free on the journey home?
Applause. Keep from a poet,
always, the slow death of his poems.

Emptying the Lake

You row the lake again
and the vee of your wake
wobbles clouds that should be geese,
disconsolate water
sucking smooth the hull
keen to be a feather
so dryly buoyant it's an island
light as the one you want
ahead but cannot always find,
that's a bush brimming from silver
-rippled rock where no one's dived,
no connections to keep up.

You land as the lake
slops up and down, a solid
your boat has made slippery.
This time you aren't staying
to unload, to take on
stillness for ballast.
No, you guide the boat
through shallows, rope it to a tree —
then take the oars again.
Dip shoulders, heave

and the island slips its moorings.
It looms, this immensity
you've unloosed.
All over its waterfront
the breeze skirmishes with sunspots.
Soon you won't need the lake,
never wanted it, and soon
the newfoundland you've towed,
Forever Island flying its pennant
of geese, is anchored.

It turns mainland overnight.

Mountains, Valleys

These whirled nights, slate
  splashdowns on our lawn
from a darker world, the roof
  straining, recall how long
tight overlapping worked.

Their lichen's spattered
  prints show hands gone under.
But what's buried holds
  things up. Roofs go on,
slates ranked in careless air.

And the tips of excavation's
  bulk of waste near here
still baulk at leverage;
  studding northern green
rollers, they have outlasted

black bergs of the south.
  So much turned inside out
in that other place translated.
  Now it's a job to find
what hasn't been ploughed in,

links gone with the chains,
  where mysterious kings
in childhood's territory
  of blackfaced men
had rearranged the earth.

After coal slid, stopping
  children dead, came levellings.
With closures, tremors
  at slack of night. Fast change
for those settlement gave grip,

pegged to ridged slopes.
  Pressure had fused them,
resisting slippage where soon
  trickles of housing
swelled the teeming coast.

In search of balance,
  mind checks its levels
for sound. Idris Davies'
  songs of the plainspeakers
named their coalscape Wrong.

Pits, slag, each chapel like
  a chapel. Style? "I don't
sell it." Style, though, it is,
  in praise of nouns dug-in,
mobilised by verbs that left,

after London wiped his eyes,
  space between poet, people,
just for his one voice.
  Yet not one only. The upland
he shared with poets, crests

where the sun had supper.
  How to sing high and low?
Hear Shelley, Rhymney, rhyme
  almost as he tried reconciling
earth voices with the sky's.

Alun Lewis above Aberdare,
  strand of a tide swinging
wide towards India,
  would have known of this.
Below, scuttled workings

measured their allotments.
  Feeling two undertows,
his sight peopled, he drifted
  where clarity's white
spread glare of promise

cleared him out. Hills blanked.
  Sun that dried his language
not heart, impaled him on himself
  when, at starvation's camp,
he left fresh bootprints.

Trying passwords still,
  he slipped connection's webbing.
Yet lives: his rescuers,
  those lines of his despatches,
struggle alone tautened.

Hills grazed just by clouds
  keep calling. Outcrops from us,
rooted, facing out, such minds
  answered for themselves.
But were trailed by roofs

where paths to the crests
  best measure distances.
Spreadeagled, the uncommon view
  can blur heart's commonplace.
Closeness though cramps vision.

So what if screens flick instant
  distances, repeat everything
worth anything's brandnew?
  Now that the balancing point
is anywhere — work dispersed

where the wronged rain falls,
  air's quarried or sea thickens —
ranks in the air press houses
  to remember. In shared
climate everyone's the weather.

Acknowledgements

Lines Review; Oxford Poetry; Planet; Poetry Wales; Red Poets; The Malahat Review; The New Welsh Review; The Use of English; The Western Mail; Drawing Down the Moon (Seren); *The Urgency of Identity* (Northeastern University Press, Chicago), and BBC Wales radio. "Biography" was written for the poetry squantum at the 1991 Hay Festival.

The sonnets in the sequence "Reading the Country" were prompted partly by poems translated from the Welsh, whose titles have been retained. The translations were found in *The Poetry of Wales 1930-1970* by R. Gerallt Jones (1970) and *Twentieth Century Welsh Poems* by Joseph Clancy (1982). The poets are:

I. T. Glynne Davies
II. Iorwerth C. Peate
III. Gwyn Thomas
IV. Gwyn Thomas
V. Gwynne Williams
VI. W.J. Gruffydd
VII. Gwilym R. Jones

VIII. T.H. Parry-Williams
IX. R. Williams Parry
X. Waldo Williams
XI. Waldo Williams
XII. T. Gwynn Jones
XIII. T.H. Parry-Williams
XIV. Euros Bowen

The author thanks the Arts Council of Wales for the award of a three-month bursary during which some of these poems were written.